Learn to Fly

Learn to Fly

Copyright © 2022 Corinne Lindsell

All rights reserved.

No part of this publication may be reproduced, distributed or transmitted in any form, or by any means, including photocopying, recording or other electronic or mechanical methods, without the prior written permission of the publisher, except in the case of brief quotations embodied in reviews and certain other noncommercial uses permitted by copyright law. The moral right of the author and illustrator has been asserted.

www.learntoflybook.com

Story: Corinne Lindsell
Illustrations: Kate Ng
Publisher: Corinne Lindsell
Design: Chris Stead, Old Mate Media
www.oldmatemedia.com

ISBN Paperback: 978-1-922740-05-2
ISBN Hardcover: 978-1-922740-06-9
ISBN Digital: 978-1-922740-07-6

Dedication

This book is dedicated to Jeffrey Lindsell, my brother. Jeffrey, you were taken in such a cruel way, and I had to learn to fly.

"Take these broken wings and learn to fly." –
(Blackbird, Lennon-McCartney)

"Take these broken wings and learn to fly"

This book is for anyone who finds themselves navigating grief and mourning.

Meet *Mystique.*

She can be annoying.

She won't go away.

Mystique is perplexing, yet persistent and, sometimes, even powerful. See that itchy bite on your left arm? That's from her.

Mozzies don't hurt you when they bite, but the touch stings afterwards. It's as if they don't mean to cause you harm.

Have you ever heard Mystique say, "this season won't last forever"?

Yes, I know. She doesn't understand that this loss is not a 'season'. This is your new reality.

Even though she means well, she is not helping.

Well, thank you for coming here: I can help you.

You may be feeling quite broken at the moment as you have a special person, a loved one, who now has wings. And it just isn't fair.

I am here for you. I was broken once, too.

Oh, I am sorry — I forgot to introduce myself.

My name is Ailis and I am going to teach you everything you need to know about learning to fly.

I haven't always been a winged creature. In fact, I used to be earthbound.

But I received wings one day, and now I am a glorious *pegasus.*

I know that you don't have wings, but you can still learn to fly. I know it is hard, but you can trust me.

You will see so many things by learning to fly.

The good thing about learning to fly is that there are only three parts to the process.

They all work together.

Are you ready?

See this teardrop?

This is called CONNECTION.

*You can touch it, you know?
It's soft like a dandelion, but strong like a medallion.*

Connection sits on the left side and is sometimes called Continued Bonds.

Connection is what you need when you hear Mystique telling you things like, "you need to let them go".

Oh, boy, I've heard this one many times myself. Mystique means well, especially when she wants you to let them go.

She doesn't want you to be in pain.

But I want you to know it is normal and healthy to stay connected to your loved one. You don't have to let them go.

Have you ever heard a song come on the radio and you've immediately thought of your loved one?

Have you ever seen a beautiful rose start to blossom on a significant day that is connected to them?

Have you ever smelt a freshly baked cake and seen their face in your mind?

Have you ever noticed a star so bright you just knew it was them?

This is connection.

These are beautiful moments through which you can continue your bond with your loved one.

Don't be afraid of these ways
to bond and continue
your connection.

They simply help you cope with
your *grief.*

And it silences Mystique when she
insists you, "let go".

Continue this bond; strengthen
this tear on your left cheek.

Now look to your right cheek.

See this beautiful teardrop? This one is as soft as a feather and as strong as a shield.

This one is called THRESHOLDS. Which means, the way through.

There will be many times when you will hear the classic Mystique word, "closure".

The problem with closure is that it implies it is finished.

This bite from Mystique can sometimes sting the most.

Think of these as the moments where you level up. Passageways you walk through with, and for, your loved one.

Afterall, you are the one trying to figure out how to keep living as the world keeps going by. Even when all you want to do is pause time, or rewind it, for just one more moment.

Thresholds are the significant moments in your life or from their life.

These are the events and milestones you never thought you'd have to experience without your loved one.

All the firsts, seconds and thirds. From the every day instances to the extraordinary moments of life. Honour these moments.

Cherish your beautiful loved one.

They are right there with you.

And when Mystique comes with her closure sting, consider it your cue to push through to that next significant moment, stronger than before.

These two *teardrops* sit side by side.

Connection to your left and thresholds to your right.

To remind you to continue the special bond you have with your loved one. Even make new ones — it is possible! And to honour your loved one as you walk through all the big and small moments of life.

You are doing a great job!

Now for the third part.

When I received my wings, I also received a new name.

It was an encounter of a whole new realm.

They called me Ailis, which means, "wings".

This name came with a very special task. I must teach people, earthbound people, how to fly. But not with wings — with tears.

So many things out there fly with natural ease; birds, butterflies, angels, fairies, dragons, bats and all kinds of insects... including our friend Mystique.

But none of these creatures have learnt the art of flying without wings.

This is my favourite part. Flying without wings is called...

TRANSCENDENCE.

Mystique may say things like, "it gets easier", or, "time will help".

But you and I both think that probably isn't true. And it definitely doesn't feel like it will ever get easier, even though she means well.

Even with time, or the idea that it will get easier, just remember there is an opportunity in every day to become more than your current feelings.

Your connections and the thresholds you walk through all serve to elevate you to a higher state.

In fact, there is a moment where they meet in the middle and it gives you a soaring strength.

Take peace, as this signifies you've begun transcending.

When you are here, you are indeed *flying.*

Learning to fly is not as simple as one, two, three. Nor does it only happen once.

This is your life's journey and it's how you'll find the **bravery** *and* **courage** *to get through every day.*

You will begin to hear Mystique say, "you are so strong".

Even when you feel the weakest you have ever felt, know that this is someone recognising you have transcended.

You will flow from your connections into your thresholds. It's a dance that moves to a *rhythm* you must write.

When both left and right find their perfect rhythm, you are moving and rising.

You will always have help to write your rhythm.

Your loved one will always help.

I can help

Even Mystique, in her annoying yet caring way, can help.

I know that you would do anything to get real wings.

But right now, you don't need them.

Even though your loved one has wings, they are probably helping someone learn how to *dance,* breathe, walk or grow through life.

Just like I was tasked to teach you how to fly.

Well, that is everything I know about learning to fly.

It may not be everything you will discover, but it's all you need to start.

May I offer you one last hint?

Embrace Mystique if you can.

She really does mean well.

Flying is the way you get through each moment, big and small, when there doesn't seem to be a way.

Flying is having these beautiful tears working together.

Flying is moving.

Flying is living.

You are ready now.

And guess what?

YOU ARE ALREADY FLYING!

About the Author

Corinne Lindsell is an accredited social worker with broad field and management experience.

Corinne's professional interests includes leadership, sustainability, grief and loss.

After the traumatic loss of her brother in 2017, Corinne was given many books and tools to help navigate grief, however she felt children's books on grief were more meaningful as it provided something simple and beautiful.

Learn to Fly is Corinne's first book, and is written to dispel the confusing dialogue out there about grief expectations, as well as challenge some of the accepted concepts.

"Corinne has put together an accessible, moving and engaging resource to guide people through arguably the worse possible trauma — the sudden loss of a loved one. Drawing on her own lived experience as well as her professional training as a social worker, Corinne's blueprint is psychologically safe, is based on solid theoretical foundations, and will have anyone affected by a traumatic loss soon enough mastering the art of flying."

— *James Boggs, Sydney*

"This book is so needed. This is a conversation about our permission to grieve. It is normalising human emotions and experiences, and provides hope to anyone who has been through trauma or who is hurting. Corinne lives and breathes healing, and now she's sharing it with the community."

— *Brianna Thomas, Clinical Psychologist*

"You will find your heart breathing a sigh of relief. Someone else GETS IT. Fuelled by a harrowing personal experience with grief, Corinne Lindsell has masterfully woven complex dynamics and simple rich imagery in this wonderful companion for all those who find themselves navigating the loss of a loved one. You'll want to return to these pages again and again as you gain the courage and strength to rise out of the pit of grief. With the help of Ailis and Mystique, you too can learn to fly."

— *Sr. Kathryn Kingsley MGL*

Endorsements

www.ingramcontent.com/pod-product-compliance
Lightning Source LLC
Chambersburg PA
CBHW041310110526
44590CB00028B/4316